From the Summit
Looking Back

Book One

ALL THE DAYS OF MY LIFE

About the Cover

SPLIT ROCK LIGHTHOUSE

During my growing-up years, Split Rock Lighthouse was a favorite family destination. Our visits often occasioned a story I heard only my father tell. The story makes son Keith's photo particularly fitting for the first book of my memoir series.

The lighthouse was a no-nonsense working facility until 1969. No fence protected the sheer cliff overlooking the lake. I walked as close to the edge as I dared to peer down on blue-green waters covering somber boulders 130 feet below. The lighthouse began operating in 1910.

It was built at the urging of ship owners following the northeaster of November 29, 1905. Worst Lake Superior storm on record, some say. It took lives and sank many ships. Among the ships that went down was the Lafayette, which gave its name to the bluff opposite Encampment Island along old U.S. 61 a few miles southwest of the lighthouse site.

Towing a 436-foot barge, the Lafayette got lost in the snow-filled darkness and smashed into the base of the bluff. The gale drove the barge into the stricken ship, breaking it in two. Miraculously, the crews of both ships survived.

Meanwhile, according to Father's story, my grandfather's half-brother, Hans, was hunkered down with his family in their rustic cabin on the lee side of the island. Secure in their beds, the family awoke to a bumping sound and felt the cabin move. Finding the door jammed, they escaped through a window and spent the night huddled in a hillside root cellar.

Morning revealed the beach swept clean, the cabin gone. For the first time in known history, waves had breached the island.

From the Summit
Looking Back

Book One
ALL THE DAYS OF MY LIFE

Lloyd Mattson

The Wordshed

Duluth, Minnesota

Cover photo and design: Keith Mattson

ISBN 0-942684-10-9

The Wordshed
Duluth, MN

Arrow Printing
Bemidji, Minnesota

To Beloved Elsie
We walked together 66 years.

MILEPOSTS

1923	Birth: August 29
1923–1927	Riverside, Duluth
1927–1941	Lester Park, Duluth
1941–1947	Bethel College and Seminary
1942–1945	Union Gospel Mission
1942	Marriage, November 19
1945	Spirit Baptist, Spirit
1947–1948	Hillsdale/West Dallas Baptist
1948–1953	First Baptist, Iron River
1953–1958	Wayside Baptist, Muskegon
1958–1962	Bethany Baptist, Anchorage
1962–1972	Baptist General Conference
1972–1977	The Between Years
1977–1986	North Shore Baptist, Duluth
1986–2002	Interim Pastorates
2002–Present	Sunset and Evening Star

CONTENTS

GOLDEN TEXTS

Continue to work out your salvation with fear and trembling, for it is God who works in you to will and act according to his good purpose.

Philippians 2:12-13

We are God's workmanship, created in Christ Jesus to do good works, which God prepared in advance for us to do.

Ephesians 2:10

We know that in all things God works for the good of those who love Him, who have been called according to his purpose.

Romans 8:28

Prologue

FROM THE SUMMIT LOOKING BACK

When I started this memoir, I envisioned a short book, a grandpa telling about the olden days. I got off to a fine start. The old codger's memory was pretty sharp, maybe too sharp. By the time I got to grade four, I was in trouble; a long book was looming. With seventy-five years worth of stories to go, I paused to reconnoiter.

I settled on two short books. The first would sketch my years with broad strokes, leaving most of the stories for Book Two. Then the Book Two folder began to bulge. OK. I'd pull the camping and outdoor stuff and put it in Book Three. Well, you get the picture: The process went on until six folders showed up in my computer. I gave them these titles:

- *All the Days of My Life.* A panoramic view of the eighty-five years.
- *Never Baptize Downstream.* Stories and vignettes from all the years.
- *By the Campfire's Ruddy Glow.* Stories about camps, camping, and the outdoors.
- *The Great Land.* Stories about Alaska and Alaskans not told in my earlier books.
- *The Making of Many Books.* Stories from years of writing, publishing, and broadcasting.
- *How Do You Know That's a Tooth?* Confessions of a happy heretic; my credo in old age.

You might think projecting six books a tad presumptuous for an octogenarian, but every tomorrow is a presumption for everyone. I figure the Lord gives each of us all the time we need to accomplish all He has in mind.

From the Summit Looking Back came from an insight I gained while resting on a boulder at Twisp Pass in the Washington Cascades late one afternoon. I was in a dark mood. I sat there studying what I could see of the trail I had just climbed. I was supposed to ride, not hike. The heavy pack I carried belonged to another man. I was out of shape, dead tired. I'll save the story for Book Three and get to the insight.

The view from the summit put my climb in perspective. I saw that the switchbacks, gullies, and steep places that wore me out were necessary inconveniences on the way to the top. There was nothing to do but keep climbing. A parable popped into mind: Just keep climbing; the trail is best discerned from the summit, looking back.

Now I have reached another summit. If you're of a mind, find a boulder and sit a spell. We'll look back on the trail together.

Introduction

A<small>LL THE</small> D<small>AYS OF</small> M<small>Y</small> L<small>IFE</small>

Surely goodness and love will follow me all the days of my life, and I will dwell in the house of the Lord forever.　　　　　　　　　　Psalm 23:6

This book takes a brisk walk through my eighty-five years. I reconstructed scenes and dialogue from memory, so I can't guarantee total accuracy, but close. I changed a few names and masked a few locations.

I learned this during those years: Life holds more than meets the eye. We connive and scheme and grumble when we don't get our druthers, but all the while, God is at work, often in hidden ways. Surely God's goodness and love followed me all the days of my life.

My walk as I wrote these chapters led through lengthening shadows and mists of sorrow. As I watched my beloved Elsie fade, the prospect of for-ever with the Lord grew ever dearer each day. By the time this book reaches you, she no doubt will be with the Lord.

For many years, God's sovereign grace has been the sustaining theme of my life. Three golden texts glowed in my heart as I revisited my 85-year ad-venture. Note the interplay of *work* and *purpose* in each of the texts:

- Philippians 2:12-13: Continue to work out your salvation with fear and trembling, for it is God who works in you to will and act according to his good purpose.
- Ephesians 2:10: We are God's workmanship, created in Christ Jesus to do good works, which God prepared in advance for us to do.
- Romans 8:28: We know that in all things God works for the good of those who love Him, who have been called according to his purpose.

No Christian need struggle to find God's will. Just keep walking. Tend to your heart, pick a direction, and head out. God will open and close doors, but He can't lead anyone who is standing still.

If you walk with God, you get where He's going. Guaranteed.

One

Roots

I was an ordinary kid from an unsophisticated, church-going family. We did not drink, dance, smoke, play cards, or go to movies, the benchmarks for Baptist piety. I had reservations about some of them, but for the most part I conformed.

Mom stayed home and ran the household. Father worked, first as a streetcar conductor then a career policeman. He rarely missed a day or arrived at the job late. I can scarcely recall an occasion when he loafed or played. After work, Father tackled jobs around home. He could fix things. No tradesmen ever darkened our door.

Father's Northern European heritage left him mostly undemonstrative. He never hugged me. Men didn't hug. He was protective, firm, and impatient with my ineptitudes, which were abundant.

Mother was gentle, but she didn't hug much either. She was just there. Brother John once commented, "If we came home and found Mom gone, we were pretty sure the rapture had occurred."

Our family attended church faithfully, grace before meals was inviolable, but we had no formal family worship. Church was not fun. Vacation Bible School (two weeks) became a summer ritual, which was about the only fun thing church offered, and much of that was not fun.

My parents' formal education never went beyond the eight grades their country schools offered. Mother read the Bible and occasional books. The newspaper and *Reader's Digest* seemed to satisfy Father's intellectual curiosity.

Father was a great storyteller, to the delight of thousands of school kids, whom he visited annually as director of Duluth's school patrol system. In old age he memorized more than 80 story poems, which he recited with vigor to all who would listen and often embellished with his harmonica.

Our family never took vacation trips. Visits to the Cotton and Kelsey farms and to relatives up the North Shore provided our family adventure. In grade school years I spent a week or more each summer on the Cotton farm, where older cousins and young uncles broadened my education.

Father was not a car man. I dimly recall a Model T with side curtains, but the car of my childhood and youth was a second-hand 1928 Chevrolet, which Father drove until 1946. Mother never drove.

At age 67 she died of a heart attack while washing dishes at home. Father remarried twice. He remained active into his 80s, then prostate cancer, Parkinson's, and heart problems took their toll. He died in a nursing home from congestive heart failure at age 89.

Father's last marriage absorbed the family assets save for a few yellow-handled tools dispersed among his sons. But our parents left a heritage of integrity, industry, and love for God. What more does one need?

Elsie's Roots

Records of Elsie's ancestry are scant. She sprang from American pioneer stock with ancestral roots in Ireland and England. She claimed that one of her ancestors founded Swedish Methodism in America; otherwise, the record reveals no religious connections.

Burton Heaton, Sr., Elsie's father, was 16 years older than his wife, Katherine. He worked as a cabinet maker and died of heart complications when Elsie was three. Her family included an older sister, Thirley, two older brothers, Burton and Ralph, and two younger brothers, Ivan and Edward. The Depression drove the impoverished widow and her brood from place to place in St. Paul.

During her final home years, Elsie lived near the Union Gospel Mission and participated in youth programs. After completing grade eight, at age 13, she was sent to work as a live-in maid.

Elsie spoke often about a striking sense of God's presence that came upon her one day while she was a child. In her teens, Simpson Memorial Church, a Christian and Missionary Alliance congregation, provided spiritual nurture. Elsie publicly confessed faith in Jesus while attending an Alliance gathering at Mission Farms near Minneapolis. In 1941, the year I came to Bethel, she enrolled at St. Paul Bible Institute.

Preston Roots

I have never spent much time digging up family roots; you never know what you might find. Grandpa Preston was quoted as saying, "When a

15

Preston moved you could be sure the constable was not far behind." Yet, a memoir demands some accounting of the gene pool.

The Prestons stemmed from American pioneer stock. There is an outside chance that one ancestor arrived on the *Mayflower*, but I wouldn't bet the farm on it. The ship manifest listed an Edward Doty, whom one source traced down to great-great-grandfather Allen Preston. Another source declared the evidence fragile. Little matter; historical records show that Doty was an unreliable, oft-sued rascal. I'd as soon lop him off the family tree.

Mayflower or no, the Prestons came from England in colonial times and lived for generations on the New World's eastern seaboard. Great-grandfather Lemuel Preston was born in 1832 in Dennysville, Maine. He moved to Potter County, Pennsylvania in 1854 and on February 27, 1864, joined the Union Army at Sharon, Pennsylvania. He served with Company G, First Regiment, Pennsylvania Light Artillery and was discharged on June 29, 1865. In 1866 he moved his family to Eau Claire, Wisconsin.

Grandfather Lorin Edgar Preston, youngest of Lemuel's large family, was born in Eau Claire in 1877. He married Lulu Adella Dunlap in 1897 and in 1902 followed his brother Amos to northeast Minnesota to seek out a homestead.

A story in the *Cotton Chronicle* by Harriet Kellner told how Grandpa Lorin rode the caboose of a freight train from Duluth to Kelsey, arriving at four on Christmas morning with the temperature a minus 30. He helped Amos build his homestead cabin east of Kelsey, then the two of them built Lorin's log cabin among magnificent white pines on the Whiteface River two miles west of the village of Cotton.

Lorin and Lulu's third child, Beatrice Lulu, was born in 1902. In 1920 she married David Jacob Mattson of Kelsey.

I remember the low-roofed homestead cabin, where great-grandma Dunlap lived her last years. I recall the somber night she died in our home. And I have good memories of the white frame house with screened porches and mysterious, dirt-floor basement that replaced the cabin.

Mattson Roots

My father's family descended from Swedes who lived in the western part of what is now Finland, before there was a Finland. Russia controlled the eastern half of the territory. In 1809 Sweden lost a war with Russia over control of the whole region. Mattson roots have been traced to the 1600s, with many second and third marriages that complicated the family tree.

Grandfather John Mattson shipped out for America at age 20 to escape conscription into the Russian military, a common practice among young Swede-Finn men. John made his way to Duluth to hunt out a half-brother, Hans.

About the same time, a group of Swede Finn girls sailed for America to sample life in the New World. Among them was Edla Hendrickson. When the other girls returned to Finland, Edla found her way to Duluth, where she too had relatives. There she met and married John and they settled among the many Swede-Finns who made their homes around the western tip of Lake Superior, a region not unlike their native Finland.

John and his half-brother Hans Mattson built houses and commercial buildings in Duluth until the economy hit a snag leading John to sign on with the Coast Guard in 1897 as a lighthouse keeper in Bayfield, Wisconsin. My father and three of his eleven siblings were born there. While in the Bayfield area, Grandfather John proved up a 160-acre homestead.

When business picked up in Duluth, the family left Bayfield and Grandfather resumed the building trade with Hans. In 1909 recession hit again and Hans bought Encampment Island and took up commercial fishing. Grandfather John bought a 40-acre farm on the Whiteface River in Kelsey Township, seven miles west of the Preston homestead in Cotton. There my father spent his youth years. Grandfather Mattson served for many years as a deputy sheriff.

Spiritual Roots

The Mattsons' evangelical fervor harks back to a pietistic movement in Northern Europe in the mid 1800s. Itinerant evangelists visited my ancestors' community; awakened believers, considering the Lutheran state church barren of life, gathered in homes to study the Bible, sing, and pray. This annoyed Lutheran officials, and they persecuted the dissenters, exiling some and leading many to seek religious freedom in America.

Three current denominations in America trace their origin to those Swedish immigrants: the Baptist General Conference, The Evangelical Free Church, and the Evangelical Mission Covenant. A fourth group, the Mission Union, made up of Finnish and Swede-Finn people, later merged with the Baptist General Conference.

Ebenezer Baptist of Duluth, a Mission Union church, began in Grandfather John Mattson's home. He led in constructing the building where the congregation worshipped for many years. The Mattsons were among the families that formed Kelsey's first church.

Grandma Preston was active in the beginnings of the Cotton Community Church. Mother's oldest sister, May, became a loyal Salvation Army member. Aunt Ethel and her husband, Carl, served the Cotton Community Church all their years and their son Kenneth continues that tradition.

I cherish good memories of Preston kin. They showed kindness to the pesky kid from the city. I came to know best Ethel and Carl Hage and their sons Kenneth, Stanley and Marty. Carl and Ethel lived out their years on the old homestead farm, our favorite Cotton haunt. I wrote tributes in verse for Carl and Ethel's home-going celebrations which will appear in Book Five.

Rev. Lloyd Hunter, a pioneer American Sunday School Union missionary, was the major influence in Mother and Father's early faith journey. He established a gospel outreach in the Kelsey-Cotton area and evangelized, baptized, and married my mother and father. They named me after him. I recall a visit by Rev. Hunter to our Duluth home when I was six or seven, a story for Chapter Two.

Rev. Hunter went from Kelsey to found the Canadian Sunday School Mission. I was honored to speak at that movement's 60th anniversary banquet. I called my talk *An Outburst of the Ordinary.*

I lauded the commitment of unheralded men and women who touched lives for God in out-of-the-way places. When the Mission published its sixty-year history, they called it *An Outburst of the Ordinary.*

While the spiritual stream of which I am a part sprang from 19th century stirrings in Europe, I am indebted to every Christian who touched my life over the years. Writing this memoir reminds me how great is that debt.

Two

A Boy's World

I was born on August 29, 1923 in St. Luke's Hospital at Duluth, Minnesota, to David and Beatrice Mattson. Sister Hazel had preceded me by a year and four months. Father was a streetcar conductor, the man who stood in back and collected fares. Mother was the quintessential homemaker. As noted in the preceding chapter, Mother and Father had grown up on subsistence farms and both had eighth-grade educations.

My childhood memories begin in a small house on Manitou Street in Riverside, a community in Duluth's far west end. I'll share some of those memories in Book Two.

In midsummer, 1927, a car whisked me away from Mother. I had no idea what was going on. After what seemed a long time, we came to a neighborhood that had real cement sidewalks—Riverside sidewalks were made of boards. On the porch steps of a small white house I saw Mother. How good she looked!

The house at 4921 Oneida Street in Lakeside had a kitchen, living room, and den, where Mother and Father slept. Hazel and I shared a small bedroom off the kitchen. The dark basement held

Mom's copper-colored, wringer washing machine, two galvanized washtubs, and a squat, black boiler that sent steam hissing and popping through iron radiators. Next door, in a larger house with crabapple trees in the yard lived a Norwegian bachelor named John Stai.

I trace my love for the outdoors to the fields and woods that stretched almost unbroken behind our Lakeside home to the Hill. Like the bear that went over the mountain, I longed to climb the Hill to see what was on the other side. Those fields and woods provided the setting for my best childhood memories. The child indeed is father to the man. These days, reminders of childhood and youth come often. We now live about six blocks from my ancestral Oneida Street home.

Days after I turned five, I enrolled in kindergarten at Lester Park School, which was four and a half blocks from home on Oneida Street. I walked those blocks four times each school day through heat, cold, rain, snow, wind, sleet, and fog. Bus kids could carry their lunch, walkers could not. I had one hour to walk home, eat, and return to class, always just at the bell.

Kindergarten memories are sketchy, though I recall a lack of talent for napping. Six elementary grades flowed smoothly, punctuated by summer vacations. I recall school friends and the Smith boys, who were not friends. I remember a few teachers clearly, but I suspect all my teachers remembered me. Our principal, Mrs. Alger, had a glorious sneeze that echoed throughout the building. We had two janitors, who wore long-sleeved blue work shirts and suspenders. They chased fragrant windrows of reddish-brown sweeping compound up and down the hardwood floors. Rumor had it that Mr. Gilbert chewed sweeping compound.

Music appreciation assemblies exposed us to Mendelssohn's Spring Song on a wind-up Victrola. Bad boys got scolded for imitating operatic sopranos.

I took part in a program in the auditorium wearing a shiny blue outfit Mother made for me. I played a real drum. And at the Christmas play I bravely recited:

I'm a little Christmas tree,
Sturdy, straight, and green.
And on my boughs at Christmas time,
Bright presents can be seen.

I was in third grade when my first circus came to town. I recall the crowd, sounds, colors, and smells. A dozen clowns climbed out of a tiny car. How did they do that? Mother pointed across the center ring. "See the elephants!" she said. I could see no elephants.

Having known no other state, I did not know how poor my vision was, nor did my parents know. They took me to a doctor who shoved a scary machine in my face and flipped little magnifying glasses in and out. He declared I had astigmatism. I became the only four-eyes in class, and for the first time I could read the blackboard and regular books. In grade four I became a habitué of Lester Park Library.

At Lester Park School a seasonal rhythm developed. In December the playground morphed into a large skating rink, and I joined the crowd in the warming shack, boys to the left, girls to the right. Big boys dared the girls' side to lace up sweethearts' skates. Acrid fumes from the coal-fired stove blended with wet wool and pipe tobacco to create a comfortable smell. Singly and in pairs, skaters circled counter-clockwise, while speedy urchins darted in and out, playing tag. A big Swede named Ole reigned over the rink. At 8:45 he blinked the floodlights, sending little kids home. At closing, volunteers pushed angled plows to clear the ice of snow and chips for the rhythmic sweep of the long fire hose.

With April came marbles. Each year a one-pound Arco Coffee can appeared on the breakfast table with my supply for the season. We played cigar, pot, span, lag, and big ring. We played for keeps, a form of gambling that could lead to no good, we were told. I learned that a fool and his marbles are soon parted, so I picked my competition with care. Yet inevitably my inventory dwindled. Drop a marble in class and you lost it. I wondered what the teacher did with all those marbles. Then came a day when my marble lust faded and I learned a lesson in Economics 101. But that story must wait for Book Two.

When I reached grade four, Father became a motorcycle cop. I would walk home from school listening for the snort of his Harley. A few times he let me ride on the radio box, which was against regulations, but sometimes a higher law prevails. The Smith boys taunted me, "You think you're smart 'cause your dad's a cop." In 1935 Father became director of Duluth's School Boy Police (no girls), a position he held until he retired 25 years later. In grade six I proudly pinned on my badge, took up my red sign and guarded the corner at

54th and Oneida. No kid dared step off the curb until I marched to the middle of the street and lifted my sign. What power!

The spring highlight was the School Boy Police picnic. Hundreds of rowdy boys boarded the side-wheeler Montauk and chugged up the St. Louis River to Fond du Lac, where they gorged on hotdogs, candy, and pop. Every kid got a pocket knife that said Duluth School Police on it. Can you imagine giving grade school kids knives to-day?

My athletic skills were dismal. I was always among the last picked when sides were chosen for ball games. However, I became a pretty fair cow-boy, in spite of a severe handicap. I excelled in dying when shot. I will tell about our cowboy wars and my handicap in Book Two.

My chief pleasures came in the fields and woods and along the crick (never creek) near our home, where I picked wildflowers and berries, built gun-nysack shacks, slept out, and cooked over open fires, often alone. I cannot explain why outdoor things so fascinated me.

About age 10 I discovered *Open Road for Boys* magazine. Deep River Jim's monthly column led to more outdoor wonders, and when the magazine announced Jim had written a book, I begged fifty cents off Father to order *Deep River Jim's Wilderness Trail Book*. A worn copy, with Jim himself hunkered by a campfire, rests on my bookshelf today, alongside a vintage Boy Scout Handbook.

At age 12 I joined Troop 18 at Lester Park Methodist Church. The legendary Scout cabin on Lavis Road rated right up there with heaven. The cabin and the Scout leaders I admired are long gone, but their impact on my life remains. Book Two will tell much more about Deep River Jim and Troop 18.

Lest you think this nothing but a geezer's inconsequential rambling, let me tell you that those boyhood adventures one day would lead to programs and writings that would touch thousands. We are indeed God's workmanship, created in Christ Jesus to do good works, which God prepared in advance for us to do.

I think often about my boyhood view of spirituality. I recall an inexplicable burst of idealism and desire to serve God that gripped me while walking home in the dark from a movie at the Lakeside Theater, a rare walk, for movies were taboo. Surely God could not speak to a boy through a movie!

Finding salvation took place through going forward. I carried a load of guilt for years because I lied to Rev. Lloyd Hunter, my parent's spiritual mentor. On a visit to our home when I was five or six, he asked me if I had Jesus in my heart. I said yes, but I had never gone forward.

I had always believed in Jesus and the Bible. Heaven and hell were part of family lore. Yet, I knew I was not saved because I had not gone forward.

My childhood church, Bethel Baptist, was tolerable but not fun. I sat with sister Hazel and my parents through interminable sermons and passed the time as best I could. Fun came in VBS and at Sunday school picnics, but otherwise, little in church life was useful. I understood perfect attendance and abstaining from the right things were the highest expressions of salvation, once you got it.

Brother John's arrival in 1932 and brother Art's

in 1934 set in motion events that would lead me to fulfill the going-forward sacrament. Mother's health was not robust after John's birth, making church attendance difficult. Hazel and I walked to Lester Park Methodist, where school friends attended.

Many Baptists held Methodists' theology suspect but I was not particular about such matters. These days, as I drive by Lester Park Church, I thank God He was not a Baptist.

It was Methodists who gave me Troop 18, Lucy Watson, the Junior Oxford League, and Red Rock Camp Meeting, where I went forward and gained salvation, at least temporarily. Methodists believed in backsliding, so you could never be sure. Baptists did not believe in backsliding, though some practiced it. The following year at Red Rock, I surrendered to preach, as they say in the South, as unlikely a candidate for the clergy as you can imagine.

At Red Rock I met Pastor Ed Rieff, whose phone call in 1941 would change my life.

Three

YOUTH YEARS

In September 1936, I enrolled at East Junior High. After seven years at Lester Park elementary, I found it a heady experience. I rode the streetcar (for a nickel). I carried my lunch. I had a homeroom, changed rooms and teachers for each class, and went to study hall (a misnomer). I managed to stay afloat in the new academic environment, signing up for all shop classes: wood turning, wood working, metal working (coal-fired forge and anvil), sheet metal, electricity, and printing. Printing was a strategic blunder.

I was among the few boys to sign up for typing class, a skill I thought might come in handy, given my penmanship. At the first class I sat behind a worn Underwood staring at blank keys. I worked on A S D F, semicolon L, K, J. A girl rushed into class late. When the teacher told her all typewriters were taken, the girl began to cry. I yielded my typewriter and headed for the print shop, where I learned to hand-set type from the California Job Case and feed a snapper press, skills already obsolete. While printing filled a class hour pleasantly, I have suffered from my compassion ever since.

After writing millions of words, I still have not mastered touch typing.

Junior Izaak Walton League was the best part of East. We met before school on Wednesdays in the gym. Coach Andy Andersen was our leader. His fly fishing demonstration fascinated me. We learned gun safety, wood lore, outdoor skills and conservation. Winters we got corn to feed grouse and in the spring, tree seedlings. In May Coach Andersen screened shaky, eight millimeter movies of the previous summer's Boundary Waters canoe trip, filling me with despair. The trip cost $25.

My half-dozen buddies became more important than family or church. We hiked, fished, camped, and discussed girls, a subject about which I lacked experience and talent. We dreamed impossible dreams, like the twelve-dollar Model T Ford. It was a fine car, but twelve dollars was hard to come by, and parental permission harder yet.

During those years I developed a trait that dogged my steps through life: Interests outside my primary duty became more compelling than the duty. I don't know how I graduated from anything. I got elected or appointed president of the Junior Oxford League at Lester Park Methodist. Then I became a Troop 18 patrol leader. I took both jobs seriously. Somehow, my school grades held to the middle of the road.

My growing involvement with Lester Park Methodist precipitated my return to the Baptist fold. Hazel had already been baptized Methodist, along with a group of her Oxford League friends. When a new Methodist pastor suggested I should join the church, since I was president of the Junior

Oxford League, my parents stepped in. We returned to Bethel Baptist, where Pastor Bill Tapper baptized me in the proper mode. I have been mostly Baptist ever since.

I sailed through Central High at C-level in generally pleasant fashion. I sang in the a cappella choir and Master Singers and played trombone in B band until my hand-me-down horn developed slide problems. My parents saw no value in a horn which could lure one into a dance band, so I gave up musicianship.

For the most part, I was an honorable student. Regular in attendance, seldom tardy, I obeyed the up-down stairway rule, except in emergencies. I suffered no discipline citations until one balmy spring day when temptation overpowered good judgment.

Before class, an open window lured three of us. We sat comfortably, our feet dangling over the drive two stories below. Without warning, my evil companions slipped inside and closed the window. Rather than disturb the class by pounding on the window, I spotted a sturdy drain pipe within easy reach. I shinnied down the drain, intending to report to class tardy but unbowed.

Unfortunately, the principal was also enjoying the balmy day. While standing at an open window on the north wing, he observed a student clambering down a drain pipe, which was contrary to school policy. On my return to class, I learned I had an appointment with the principal. He was stern but reasonable. Because of my untarnished record, he assessed only two days suspension.

Thinking it prudent not to discuss the matter with my parents, I spent the suspension in the

Boys' Y across from the school studying and plotting revenge. Months later, Mother commented dryly on the incident. Who ratted, I do not know.

On graduation day my name appeared well down the class roster. I donned cap and gown and marched to "Pomp and Circumstance," but with growing apprehension. I had declared my intent to enter Bethel Junior College in September, but I had scarcely a dollar to my name, no prospect for help from home and no job. I had heard about miracle letters that arrived just in time with exactly the amount needed, but that seemed shaky ground for funding college. I hoped Bethel Church might cough up a few bucks for ministerial trainees, but all I got were pats on the back.

A night job opened at Ralph's Standard Service on London Road at 35 cents an hour, but for the first and last time in my life, I failed a boss's expectations and got fired. College was 11 weeks off. Jobs were hard to come by. Frustration led me to a thoughtless, impetuous act. Without telling my parents and with less than three dollars, I hitchhiked to Minneapolis to hunt out Swedish Methodist Hospital, where I heard Bethel students often worked.

Red Rock Camp was in session at Medicine Lake on the Minneapolis outskirts. With friends there, I was confident I could stay a day or two while I checked out the job. I found a bus to Medicine Lake and the manager offered lodging and meals in exchange for a few hours' work. I phoned home to worried parents.

The next morning I took a bus to town and found the hospital. A kind man told me he had no summer openings but to check back in the fall.

With no other job prospects in mind, I bought a sack of crabapples for a dime, found a bus to the north end of town near highway 61 and headed home.

The trip gave me time to think. I knew about the city employment agency but feared there would be a fee. I was down to one dime. My last ride dropped me off downtown and I located the employment agency. Relieved to learn there was no fee, I met with a no-nonsense woman who took my work history, shuffled papers, and said. "This just came in." The Direct Service Gas Station on West Superior Street was looking for an experienced man. I walked the mile to the station, nailed the job, and used my last dime for a bus fare home.

Direct Service was a fun place to work, a congenial boss and crew. The job paid the usual 35 cents an hour, an extra nickel for night shift, and ten percent commission on accessory sales. By working every hour they would give me and nights whenever possible, money slowly accumulated. I sold tires and accessories aggressively, but by August it became evident I would not have enough money for college.

The thought of deferring college a year began to grow. I would work hard and save. Possibly I could buy a cheap car, maybe enjoy an occasional date. That seemed the way to go, but pride kept me from sharing my thoughts.

I was working the drive one morning when the boss called, "Phone, Lloyd." I heard a familiar voice. "This is Pastor Rieff. I've been thinking about you. How is it with your soul?" Without hesitation I replied, "Everything's fine, Pastor Rieff. I'm heading for Bethel in a couple weeks." I hung up the phone and gave the boss notice.

Forty years later, while serving North Shore Church in Duluth, I learned that Pastor Rieff still lived in the area. He was long retired. I invited him to speak at our Sunday evening service and introduced him with the story of his phone call. He admitted he didn't remember. I suspect he had made many such calls in his long ministry, but surely no call was more Spirit-led.

Four

BETHEL COLLEGE AND SEMINARY

Mom cried when we hugged goodbye under the apple tree in our back yard. My steamer trunk was already aboard Dad's '28 Chevrolet. She stood watching as we drove off for the Union Depot.

Dad helped carry my luggage into the train station. I paused, thinking he might buy my ticket, but he walked on. At the train he put out his hand, his eyes misting. "Well, so long, Dad," he said. He had been playing our farewell in his mind. He laughed sheepishly, shook my hand, and left without looking back.

In St. Paul I hired my first cab. I barely knew where Bethel was, and I did not know enough to tip the cabbie. He dropped me off at the two-story brick building on North Snelling Avenue. I was at Bethel! I had turned 18 a week earlier.

Registering and settling in took three days and all my money but pocket change. On the fourth day, I rode a streetcar to the State Capitol. I started walking west on University Avenue, hitting every business that might possibly hire part-time help.

A sign on a bowling alley window beckoned. Pinsetters Wanted. I had never bowled in my life. The manager said on a good night I could make as much as three dollars! I told him I'd be back if I found nothing else. Two miles and many stops later, I came to Lexington Tire and Battery Company. The owner, Mr. Gibbs, hired me to work weekdays from four to nine and Saturdays from noon to closing. The pay: 35 cents an hour. It was a good job.

One afternoon Mr. Gibbs took me along to deliver a load of tires to a trucking firm. On the way back we stopped at the Blue Lagoon, a tavern on Mississippi Street. He bought me a Coke and pointed out a painted lady plying her trade. No way could I have imagined that the following summer I would build a kids' playground on the lot behind the Blue Lagoon.

In December a new Mobile station on Como and Snelling, walking distance from school, advertised for help. I could save an hour's commute and 15 cents carfare each workday. I got the job for 35 cents an hour.

Work left little time for study and no time for dating. I made the Bethel Male Chorus, but work kept me from performances, so I dropped out. My studies went reasonably well, considering. I ate breakfast and lunch in the school coffee shop and supper at a small restaurant next to the Mobile station.

The new quarter found me in President Wingblade's office asking for an extension on tuition. That became a pattern. I do not know how I managed finally to square up.

On December 8 I joined a somber group in the gym listening to President Roosevelt's "Day of Infamy" speech on a tinny radio. We all carried Selective Service cards. Pre-seminary students could claim 4D exemption, but I was not comfortable with that.

The Mobile station job worked out well until a December blizzard blew in. With both service bays taken, I lay on the drive under a pickup, snow creeping under my jacket. My job was to guide a battery into its carrier while my boss lowered it from above. Tolerances were close, forcing me to remove my mitts. The boss, not the world's best mechanic, dropped the battery on my bare fingers. The thought crossed my mind: there must be an easier way to earn a living.

Perhaps that's why the note on the school bulletin board caught my attention. A blind man named Ed Ferrell was seeking a live-in companion to run errands and cook breakfast and supper. He offered unspecified compensation plus room and board. Confident I could learn to cook, I took the job.

I found Ed friendly but penurious. The compensation turned out to be a grudging ten bucks a month. I cooked tolerably well and packed myself generous lunches. I slept on a miserable folding bed in the living room and studied at the kitchen table. But Ed's growing demands left little time for study and he increasingly begrudged any time away except school hours.

One evening I took Ed by streetcar to a Spiritualist meeting where healings allegedly occurred. He was Catholic, but he saw no harm in covering the bases. Ed didn't get healed, but we did get free readings. Mine warned me to look out for a blonde.

A woman of indeterminate years and acquired red hair invited us to her apartment for refreshments. She told spooky stories about spirits playing tricks. We heard mysterious rappings. "Oh, they're here!" she said.

Radiator, I concluded. I began to question how long I wanted to stay with Ed.

Then, destiny. A classmate named Ken whose economic status paralleled mine worked afternoons and evenings at the Ober Boys Club, an outreach of the St. Paul Union Gospel Mission in a predominately black neighborhood. The club was a half-mile or so from Ed Ferrell's apartment, and Ken invited me to drop in for a visit. The facility and program impressed me. I envied Ken. Student employees received ten dollars a month and room and meals in the Mission's commercial hotel and restaurant.

For many years, the Mission had operated the St. Paul Boys Club in its downtown building, but it was closed for want of a director.

Ken was keeping company with a mission volunteer named Lou. Early in January he proposed a Saturday double date. We would take in a Bethel basketball game, followed by a visit to the Port Arthur, a downtown café noted for low prices. He promised to find me a date. Having been at Bethel four months with no social life whatever, his proposal sounded good.

On date night, over Ed's objection, I walked to the Mission. Turned out, Ken had had a spat with Lou. He introduced me to his date, a perky St. Paul Bible School student named Elsie, who worked at Rudin Pharmacy, a business in the Mission building. Then he introduced me to Nelly, a tall, blonde high school girl who showed no enthusiasm for me whatever. I perceived she had her eye on Ken.

We caught a streetcar to Bethel, where we lost the game and I lost ground with Nelly. The chill

37

deepened at the Port Arthur. While we waited in a booth for our food, Elsie announced for the powder room. She took Nelly with her, and I told Ken what I thought of his matchmaking.

When the girls returned to the booth, Elsie wore a foxy grin. "We decided to swap boyfriends," she said, and sat down close to me. The evening warmed. I saw Elsie home by streetcar to Mounds View, where she roomed. I thanked her for saving the evening and asked if I could see her again. She agreed, but surrendered no goodnight kiss. Being a novice in such matters, I failed to get her phone number.

Two weeks went by. The St. Paul Winter Carnival was on. I thought the Saturday parade would provide a cheap occasion to connect with Elsie, but with no home phone number, my plan collapsed. On Saturday morning, ignoring Ed's protest, I threw on my black overcoat and headed downtown on foot.

The parade crowd was gathering. Masked Vulcans roamed the sidewalks, kissing unresisting ladies. In a despondent mood, I picked my way along the parade route to Wabasha Street, brushing by families bundled against the Minnesota cold. At Wabasha I turned north, with no particular destination in mind. A short distance up Wabasha, a cluster of giggling girls stood on a low porch waiting for the parade. We spotted each other at the same time. We hugged. Elsie wondered how I found her. So did I.

Five

Union Gospel Mission

Elsie compounded my problems with Ed because cultivating a romance takes time and he was growing increasingly demanding. I contemplated changing jobs, but I had held three jobs in five months, and given my schedule, I saw no options that would improve my lot. Then destiny kicked in again.

Glen Dewey directed the Ober Club. When Ken mentioned I was from Duluth, Glen invited me to stop by to chat. He too was from Duluth.

Glen told me his parents had led Duluth's rescue mission for many years. A cop named Mattson had faithfully supported the work. Glen wondered if I might be related to him. Figure that out. At the close of our conversation, Glen invited me to join the Ober Club staff.

I walked back to Ed's barely touching the ground. In the space of three weeks I had found a girlfriend and a dream job. I gave Ed a week's notice and moved to a cubicle on the fourth floor of the Mission building. The restaurant served good food and packed noon lunches. The monthly ten-dollar stipend scarcely mattered; I would get to see Elsie almost every day.

Then destiny moved up another notch. Peter MacFarlane (Mac), a legendary rescue mission leader, was eager to reopen the downtown club. He tapped me. With no training, and only three months experience at Ober Club, I found myself directing the St. Paul Boys Club (later named the Arthur H. Savage Club for Boys).

I learned later that Elsie's older brothers had attended the club, and she too had been involved in Mission programs.

I worked at the club from 3:30 to 9:00 weekdays, with an hour's break for supper. The club facility included an office, prayer room, game room with fireplace, library, craft room, print shop, woodwork shop and gymnasium. I worked alone to begin with, but as attendance grew, I was allowed to recruit for crafts and the gym.

My job description included the Sunday afternoon Sunday school and evening service. I inherited the Sunday school bus, a modified Model A flatbed with retired streetcar seats. I had Saturdays off, but Elsie gravitated to the Mission on her free time and I had little incentive to be elsewhere.

After a few months on the job, I persuaded Mac I needed office help. I suggested offhand that the girl who worked for Rudin Pharmacy might do. Mac knew Elsie from her childhood involvement in the mission. For a short time she had operated the Mission elevator. Mac allowed me to hire Elsie and assigned her a room well down the women's wing of the hotel. Thus began our life together in Christian service.

When the spring quarter at Bethel ended, I plunged into Mission work full-time, gaining a modest pay increase. My first assignment was to revive a playground outreach on a weedy lot off Mississippi Street behind a tavern called the Blue Lagoon. That's a Book Two story.

Afternoons often found me at Snail Lake Camp just north of St. Paul, preparing for the summer program. I frequently needed Elsie's help. Each night I took part in the street meeting on the Mission corner, where I tormented passersby with my trombone.

I worked parts of four years for the mission, gaining varied and valuable experiences. In many respects, the Mission contributed more to my education than did Bethel. Some of our many Mission adventures will be told in Books Two and Three.

Six

The Girl that I Married

The summer of '42 passed swiftly, and my court-ship of Elsie progressed favorably. The Mission became our home, church, and family. We travelled about on foot, by streetcar, and bicycle. Riding your girl on a bike is most pleasant. The old Mission bus took us to Snail Lake Camp often for projects, real or imagined. See "A Bucket of Bullheads," Book Two.

Elsie was not hard to please. The daughter of a Depression widow with six children, at age 13 she was sent from home to work as a live-in maid and nanny. In late summer I took her by train to Duluth to show her off. She caught a nice lake trout near Encampment Island and I caught none.

The war was casting a pall over the land when I enrolled for my sophomore year at Bethel. I cranked up the boys club program. I coached eleven tough kids to the St. Paul playground league football championship, which ate up Saturdays. All the while, I felt the military draft blowing down my neck.

Rumor had it that enlistees were given some choice in military assignment. I thought maybe I could become a chaplain's assistant. The thought built momentum, and convinced I would not be around to complete my sophomore year, I withdrew from Bethel to work full-time at the Mission.

I had grown increasingly protective of Elsie. She was essentially alone. Young love and the uncertainties of the time led me to a rash decision: I suggested to Elsie that we marry. I would enlist and send her my pay. She would take an apartment, get a job, and wait out the war.

Friends warned us we were too young and immature for marriage. It would never last. They were right, of course, but we managed. We celebrated our 66th wedding anniversary in November 2008.

On November 19, 1942, Pastor George French married us in the Simpson Memorial Church parsonage. Elsie's brother Burt and his wife, Lucy, were our witnesses. When I gave Pastor French five dollars for his services, he had more money than I did. Burt treated us to our wedding dinner at the Port Arthur Café. Most fitting.

I presumed on my parents in Duluth to put us up while I worked on enlistment, which I assumed would take but a short time. Then I learned there was a pre-induction screening. While waiting for that, I found a job on the bull gang at Zenith Shipyards building Coast Guard ships for an incredible 78 cents an hour! I joined a bawdy crew of rowdies.

One stormy holiday the gang boss called us in to clear snow. Double time! When the wind-chill turned dangerous, the idiot sent us home. I'd have worked outdoors naked for $1.56 an hour.

The shipyard job ran out in January. I then worked mornings and afternoons as a plumber's helper and evenings at a garage. When the screening finally took place in mid-February, my plan fell apart. My vision rendered me ineligible for enlistment. They said I would be drafted, but for limited service.

Leaving Elsie in Duluth, I returned to St. Paul to look for an apartment and a job. I found a second-floor apartment not far from the Mission for $35 a month and a job at a Direct Service station, a mile from the apartment. Two days later I met Elsie at the train depot and we walked hand in hand to our first home.

The apartment included kitchen appliances; that was it. At a Goodwill Store two blocks from the apartment we bought a bed with a reasonably clean mattress, a four-drawer dresser, worn sofa with matching chair, kitchen set with two chairs, pots, pans, and table service. We had money for only one knife.

Passersby probably thought it strange to see a young man carrying bedsprings, mattress, and sofa down the sidewalk on his back.

Uncle Sam's greetings came in mid-August. I kissed a tearful Elsie, now pregnant, and boarded a streetcar. At Fort Snelling I joined a long line of naked men who moved from station to station. A doctor ordered me to turn my head and cough. Cough again. He scrawled a red X across my folder. Hernia. 4F. I was stunned and elated. A stroke of a pen moved me from the shipyard bull gang to physically unfit for military service.

I rode the streetcar home to Elsie with a light heart and shortly after, I enrolled at Bethel for my sophomore year.

My life has been marked by rash decisions. We were anticipating our first baby in November. I had been promoted to manage a Direct Service station nearer our apartment. My route home took me by the Mission, and curious to learn how the Club was doing, I stopped in. I met the new director, Ted Nickel. The sounds and smells and greetings from kids got to me. I asked Ted if he could use another man.

Soon I was back at the Mission for considerably less pay than the service station provided, and that fact would rise to haunt me. Sally was born on November 4 at Bethesda Hospital in St. Paul. After the obligatory week-long stay, I came for my wife and baby, $100 shy of the hospital bill. I promised to pay up the next Friday, payday at the Mission. I got a steely smile: full pay or no wife and baby.

I headed for Elsie's brother Burt to seek a loan. He laughed. The only money he had was the packing house football pool, and no way would he loan me that. If he showed up Monday morning without the pool money, the men would kill him. It took a while, but I left with $100, mostly in coins. I hurried on foot to the hospital to ransom Elsie and baby Sally. On Friday I paid Burt, leaving me $20.

I don't recall how we made it until the next pay check, nor do I know how we survived the next three years. Landlords got cranky over late rent; we were often short of food. When carfare ran out, I hitchhiked or biked to school. There were days I lacked change to make a phone call, but we muddled through.

After Sally came, we found a larger apartment on Marshall Street near the Cathedral, a long walk to the Mission. My homeward route took me by

Mickey's Diner where I could buy six small hamburgers for a quarter. Many nights after closing the club, I would buy six, sometimes 12, tuck them under my coat, and run up the hill to our apartment.

One night a scream woke me. On the night stand between our bed and Sally's crib, not a foot from Elsie's nose, sat a harmless mouse nibbling on crumbs.

In September 1944, I began my second year at seminary, struggling to balance studies with home and work duties. Somehow, I managed to keep out of the dean's office. Then in May, as the school year wound down, I made another rash decision. I signed up for a summer student pastorate, a common practice among seminarians. Spirit Baptist Church in North Central Wisconsin invited me to serve June through August. The pay would be $100 a month.

•

Seven

SPIRIT
1945

The summer pastorate at Spirit must rank near the top of my list of irresponsible decisions. We gave up a comfortable apartment and my job at the Mission. Sally was a toddler. We had no car, and I was flat broke.

Used cars were scarce but I found a 1931 Chevrolet for 600 borrowed dollars. No one knew how many miles the car had, but the rubber looked fair and it had a trailer hitch.

On the first Saturday of June, I rented a nondescript trailer and loaded our gear plus luggage belonging to two VBS teachers, who would ride with us. I pointed the Chevy toward Spirit 200 miles away, expecting to arrive by early evening.

We arrived three days and four flats later, having exhausted our money and most of the VBS teachers' money. See Book Two, "The Poor in Spirit."

Farm fields lush with new crops surrounded the small white church. A tiny kitchen and bedroom in the church became our summer home. Church families looked after the VBS teachers. We hauled water from a farm across the road in a five-gallon milk can. An ancient outhouse next to the woodshed out back welcomed us.

The handle of the axe wedged in the chopping block by the woodshed suffered damage one day when I challenged Elsie to hit it with a .22. She scared a mouse half to death in the far corner of the kitchen with the same .22. Elsie was a regular Annie Oakley.

The congregation treated us warmly. Invitations for meals came often and a family included us on Sunday afternoon picnics and fishing at a nearby river. I relieved Pearson Lake of slab-sized crappies. Potlucks on the church grounds filled occasional Sunday afternoons. Book Two will include Spirit stories, including the Green Lantern episode, and a night-time jaunt that nearly turned deadly.

At the end of August, the church asked if I would continue with them through Christmas, commuting from St. Paul. They offered $25 per Sunday, including travel. I drove the Chevy until snow came, then rode the Soo Line, which ate up half my weekly pay. In January I joined the Seminary pulpit supply pool, riding buses to Minnesota churches on weekends.

On our return from Spirit, we found an apartment near the Selby streetcar line. Finding work that fit my school and weekend schedule was difficult. I settled for a bellhop job at the Lowry Hotel, a fading downtown establishment. I worked from six to eleven.

Toting booze to rooms posed a dilemma for a bone-dry Baptist, but the tips were good and I figured the Lord would understand. Keith arrived on

December 27, 1945, and this time I found the money to spring Elsie and baby.

In January a job opened at Joe's Diner, an eight-stool greasy spoon a few blocks from our apartment. I figured I could learn to be a fry cook. I worked alone Tuesday through Friday from five to closing at ten, then hurried home to hand-wash diapers, easing Elsie's load a little.

In September I began my final year of seminary. I worked where I could and preached most Sundays. We were without a car, so Elsie had to stay home with Sally and Keith. Her patient heroism through school years and beyond qualifies her for eternal sainthood.

Eight

HILLSDALE/WEST DALLAS
1947-1948

As my final year in seminary unfolded, a fear that had long lurked in a far corner of my mind began to stir. What if, having finished seminary, no church wanted me? In December 1946, a neatly written letter on blue-grey stationery eased that fear.

Hillsdale and West Dallas Baptist churches, small American Baptist Convention congregations in North Central Wisconsin, inquired if I would consider candidating. I replied with undignified haste.

On the appointed weekend, I rode a Greyhound to Barron, where Harold Lowe, a tall, thin farmer from the Hillsdale church, met me. His immaculate Model A coupe took us to a tidy dairy farm, where his comely, short wife, Lita, greeted me. She called me Reverend.

I first visited the West Dallas church, a small, rectangular building surrounded by snow-covered fields. Eight adults greeted me. They formed a half-circle around the wood stove well back in the auditorium. An elderly woman moved to the piano, which needed tuning. She accompanied several hymns, every chord an arpeggio. When I mounted the platform to preach, I could see my breath.

Why didn't I join the circle by the stove and

preach sitting down? Young guys bent on making an impression don't do that.

After the sermon, we talked about my family and personal interests. Then someone drove me about two miles to Hillsdale.

The church had a square bell tower. Seven board steps led up to the foyer. Perhaps 40 people listened politely to my sermon, and a smaller number returned in the evening for another sermon and discussion. I rode the bus back to St. Paul Monday morning feeling good.

The call came on the same blue-grey stationery. The Hillsdale church offered a parsonage and $100 a month. West Dallas offered $50 a month. My acceptance hit the afternoon mail.

Through the winter and spring I commuted by Greyhound to the churches, often accompanied by Sally, a gregarious three-year-old who chatted with bus passengers and charmed the congregations. Elsie would not see the churches until late spring, when we bought another '31 Chevy, borrowing $475. Driving a 16-year-old car did not trouble me. My father ran his '28 Chevy until 1946.

In mid-May a farm truck moved us to our first parsonage: five rooms and a sun porch. The basement held a chemical toilet that promised winter comfort. The path to the outhouse was well worn. A grim hot-air furnace gobbled fuel our one winter there. I scrounged wood and bought coal one gunnysack at a time from the feed mill. Our water came from a clunky outdoor pump jack which froze in early winter.

About two dozen families lived in Hillsdale, with handsome dairy farms scattered in all directions. The town included a general store, a two-pump gas station, an auto repair garage that operated off and on, a six-stool coffee shop, feed mill, and pickle factory. Other buildings included a tiny telephone exchange, town hall, two-room school, and two churches.

West Dallas Church was dying—I would be its last pastor. A handful of adults and a few children attended morning worship. A few more children showed up for Sunday school following the service. Hillsdale had about 40 members with additional non-members attending regularly. Farm families and retired folks composed both congregations.

We served the churches for only 20 months, and some good things happened, especially in West Dallas. That became my undoing. I had not learned a fundamental principle: when serving two churches, never report successes in one you can't match in the other. I learned another lesson: Never baptize downstream. See Book Two for those stories.

I officiated at more funerals in Hillsdale than in any parish that followed. I was the township's only resident pastor. A primitive form of hospice placed elderly welfare patients with local widows. The caregivers often turned to me when the patients died. Funerals became community events; some were downright remarkable.

Joel was born in Rice Lake on December 11, 1947. Elsie found the pregnancy and birth difficult, and the hospital bill compounded my growing financial problems. Then Chevy II died from my attempts to repair loose connecting rods. The car had doubled as a church bus, once carrying ten kids.

Getting to West Dallas Sunday mornings became a problem. When I asked a church elder, who lived across the street from the parsonage, if he would drive me, his wife declared, "We ain't running no taxi service." My Sunday morning walk was less than two miles and a West Dallas friend drove me to Hillsdale for the eleven o'clock service.

Sunday mornings at West Dallas frustrated me from the beginning. I met the kids only in passing. I proposed that we combine Sunday school and worship and the congregation bought the idea. I led a lively song service, then taught the teens and adults. Two children's classes met in opposite corners of the small auditorium, moving outdoors when weather allowed.

Attendance grew immediately. More parents came. Kids brought their friends, who loved riding in my Chevy. The VBS in June found the church crawling with kids, a new experience for the church. Several kids professed faith in Jesus and I planned the first baptismal service West Dallas had witnessed in decades and the first of my career. That baptism gave Book Two its name.

My undoing began the Sunday West Dallas counted more heads than Hillsdale. I was stupid enough to report the fact. Then someone sent a report to the Convention office and an exaggerated, flowery write-up appeared in the district newsletter, sealing my doom.

Persistent debt added to my woes. West Dallas occasionally fattened its monthly check, but the prospect for a raise from Hillsdale stood somewhere below zero. When a letter came from First Baptist in Iron River, Michigan, inviting me to candidate, I gladly accepted. It was a bigger church in a bigger town, and it belonged to the Baptist General Conference, my ancestral denomination. I notified the churches of my intention and waited.

Nine

IRON RIVER, MICHIGAN
1948-1953

Iron River was a mining town of about 5,000 on U.S. 2, in Michigan's Upper Peninsula. It was about 200 miles from Hillsdale. Getting there posed a problem. I had no car, bus connections were poor, and I was close to broke. I opted to hitchhike.

Early Saturday morning I walked to Highway 25 carrying an overnight bag. I hoped no parishioner would see me. A trucker stopped. When I told him my destination, he said I was in luck. He was heading for Hurley, a town on the Wisconsin/Michigan border half way to Iron River. I had never heard of Hurley.

The trucker dropped me off at a Standard Oil Station and I looked up the phone number of Paul Obinger, a pastor friend in neighboring Ironwood. I hoped we might have coffee and I could pick his brain about Iron River. Getting no answer, I picked up my bag for the short walk to U.S. 2.

A well-dressed woman approached me, probably noting my lack of a vehicle. She asked if I would care to visit her place of business for refreshments. Something told me that would not be a good idea. When I explained I was a minister hitchhiking to Iron River, her tone changed to amusement and she offered to drive me on through three adjacent towns to the open road on U.S. 2. We rode in the fanciest car I had ever been in. An angel in disguise? I don't think so.

I reached Iron River by late afternoon and hunted out the Gamble Store, where I was to meet my contact, Arnold Sjodin. I suspect he guessed I had hitchhiked, though he didn't comment. Arnold would remain a friend throughout his life.

The candidating process went comfortably. I loved the old church, the two-story parsonage next to the church, and the countryside. I noted many kids and young people in the congregation and was sorry Elsie wasn't with me.

The church provided a generous honorarium, but instead of waiting for a late Monday evening bus, I hitched to Duluth. I spent the night with my parents and caught a bus to Cameron, a town near Hillsdale. Elsie arranged for a friend to pick me up.

The call came in a letter from Bill Cook, church clerk. The church offered the parsonage and $200 a month. The $50 a month increase over my present salary sounded enormous. I hadn't calculated the cost of heating an old, uninsulated house. Nor had I figured out how I would serve the scattered congregation without a car.

We said goodbye to Hillsdale and West Dallas. A few friends wept. The Iron River church sent a truck for our furnishings and a car for the family. We moved to our second parsonage with Sally, Keith, and Joel.

HILLSDALE AND WEST Dallas had taught me a

great deal about pastoring, but Iron River was to provide the seminal experiences for my career. The church seemed generally healthy, but the scars typical of our ethnic-rooted congregations were evident. Its history revealed recurring squabbles and major upheavals, the most recent soothed by Minnie Nelson, one of the few woman pastors tolerated in the Conference.

Minnie served in Iron River from 1938 until 1945. She brought healing and modest growth. A seminary classmate, Bob Paulson, followed Minnie and stayed two years. I would be next.

During Bob's tenure, several families new to Iron River joined the church. Among them were Ed and Louetta Cole and Arnold and Opal Sjodin. They deserve the credit for the good work the Lord did during my five years in Iron River.

Ed managed the Montgomery Ward store and Arnold managed Gambles. Tough business competitors, they became close friends and provided strong leadership in our church and the broader Christian community. And they looked after Elsie and me.

I remember most Iron River people fondly, others not so fondly. The latter, however, taught me a vital principle for pastoring: When fighting a heavyweight, clinch a lot. If you stay close, he or she can't slug you.

Serving the church without wheels was next to impossible, but buying a car was off the radar. When a church member offered to help, I counted it an answer to prayer. The help was an interest-free $600 loan to buy a 1936 Hudson Terraplane owned by a former pastor. The mileage was anyone's guess. I drove the car about 3,000 miles before it died along U.S. 2 near Watersmeet. I still owed the $600.

Harold Lindahl, the local Chevrolet dealer, with the connivance of Arnold Sjodin, I suspect, arranged financing for a new Chevy for a shocking $2,000. He allowed $95 for the dead Terraplane and never got it running. That left me with two cars to pay for.

Iron River was a study in contrasts. I had the finest youth group of all our years, and the most cantankerous cluster of old folks. But the joy the kids brought far outweighed the misery wrought by a few old Swedes. Book Two will tell the story.

PROVIDENTIALLY, GOD'S INVASION Army (GIA) came to Iron River the fall I arrived. Founded by Pastor Ed Nelson, GIA recruited post high school youths for a year of evangelistic outreach. Teams fanned out among Conference churches to conduct children's meetings, do door-to-door evangelism, and present inspirational programs.

GIA inspired our young people with its enthusiasm and spiritual depth. Several children and youths professed faith in Christ, including our Sally, then five years old. Some of our young people served with the ministry.

The following year a GIA team came to work in neighboring Crystal Falls. The goal was to revive a Bible study launched a few years earlier and explore the community for a possible new church. Iron River young people helped with children's meetings, meeting in a lodge hall.

GIA members canvassed the town, the Bible study resumed, and through the fall and winter I met with the group on Thursday evenings in the

Seventh Day Adventist Church. Joel often came with me. He sang his first solo, "It is No Secret", to the handful of people. He returned 43 years later to sing the same song at Faith Baptist Church of Crystal Falls, the outgrowth of the humble Bible study.

BIBLE CAMP WAS another growth factor during our Iron River days, thanks largely to Bill Cook. Bill was a mailman, faithful church member, and tireless camp booster. Bible Camp Bill, we called him. He not only recruited campers, he nudged adults to volunteer as kitchen staff and cabin counselors.

The Upper Michigan Conference rented Camp Bird, a Forestry Department facility near Crivitz, Wisconsin, for two weeks each summer. Thanks to Bible Camp Bill, Iron River frequently carried home the most-campers trophy. It was at Camp Bird that I first met Lawrence Swanson, a godly man we will encounter in chapters to come.

Elsie and I were 25 when we came to Iron River. Sally and Keith began school there, and David was born in nearby Stambaugh on December 10, 1950. Elsie drove young people to St. Paul for Bethel prospective student days. She hosted get-togethers in the parsonage. I sat through chilly football games and hunted and fished with the boys and men. I promised campouts to junior boys who behaved themselves in VBS. No boy ever failed to qualify. Sunday mornings, I picked up a carload of kids for Sunday school.

Our young people presented monthly programs at the Gibbs City Transient Camp, a home for old lumberjacks, and the Iron County Infirmary. For a time we conducted a Sunday afternoon meeting in the village of Amasa.

When Iron River's first radio station went on the air, we got involved at several levels. I launched *Melodies of Life,* a half-hour Saturday night broadcast that ate up time and energy but touched a few lives significantly.

Our years in Iron River were busy and blessed, but the gloom of debilitating debt hung over me. I grew increasingly restless, and when Wayside Baptist Church of Muskegon, Michigan, invited me to candidate, I thought perhaps it was time to move on.

Ten

MUSKEGON
1953-1958

Once again I had to leave Elsie home when I went on a candidating visit. Funds were too low for a family trip. I took a bus to Manitowoc, Wisconsin, and rode the ferry across Lake Michigan to Muskegon, an industrial city of about 40,000. A fellow ferry passenger drove me to the church, a trim, white chapel in a community of fine homes. Lincoln Elementary School stood across McCracken Street to the west. Across from it was a small grocery store.

The congregation responded kindly to my preaching; the pulpit committee discussion was positive. My host gave me a quick tour of the town, and we stopped by the parsonage. It contrasted sharply with our aging, cold Iron River home. Wayside grew more appealing by the minute. The church bought me my first commercial plane ride back home, which impressed me. The call came shortly, and we began the farewell process, which was not easy.

The night before moving day, I slipped alone into the old church, where God had touched hearts, including mine. I stepped to the pulpit where I had preached hundreds of sermons. I knelt by the pew where I had heard confessions of faith. In that staid room I had baptized, married and buried adults and kids. I had dedicated children and conducted a miracle wedding. I had been scolded and hugged.

I had come to Iron River five years earlier with no agenda but to be a pastor. I would leave remembering forever what God had wrought. I prayed and cried.

On a Monday morning I loaded the family in our blue Chevrolet and drove to the Straits of Mackinac, where we slept to a pile driver lullaby. Construction was under way on the bridge. The ferry across the Straits gave us our first ride on a big boat.

We started early the next morning and drove south through groomed orchards, farmlands, and woodlands. I loved the countryside. We reached the Wayside parsonage in early evening in August 1953. Kevin joined the family on October 11, 1955. We spent five good years at Wayside.

A period of tension had depleted attendance somewhat, but the auditorium soon began to fill and the Sunday school grew. It became obvious we had to add space.

Muskegon was a lively town with broad interchurch involvements. Historic Maranatha Bible Conference was near the church. I got involved in two pastor fellowships and involvements began to pile up. I had not yet learned that just because you can do something doesn't mean you should. My old nemesis, debt, continued to haunt me.

In keeping with the scope of this book, I will parcel out good stories to future books and sketch briefly the activities that occupied my heart and time.

The church tackled the space problem. We negotiated the use of Lincoln School's gymnasium for Sunday mornings and began planning an addition to church.

About that time, Wayside sponsored a German family displaced by the war. Henry and Anna Bansen came with their two children bringing a rewarding experience to church life. Our contractor hired Henry, a skilled craftsman, to work on the church addition.

Prior to the building project, I had launched a Monday night boys' program. We accepted kids of any age, and dads showed up to help. We made kites and knickknack shelves, ice fishing poles and bird houses. Kids from the community began to come. It was a fruitful program, but the building program wiped it out.

Then a new family joined Wayside. Joe Burkhart came to teach science at Lincoln School. When I learned he had been in Scouting, I saw a way to relieve the boys' work deficit. Working with Joe, the school, and the Boy Scout Council, we put together a program. Joe agreed to be scoutmaster, I signed on as chaplain, and within a year we had 60 boys in the troop and about 100 in the Cub Pack. The committee bought and refurbished a used bus and the troop enjoyed dream trips. Book Three will tell the mostly-true story from one trip, "Joe and the Gypsy Fortune Teller."

Somewhere in all this I stumbled into a hitch with WMUS, Muskegon's Christian radio outlet. What began as a short-term position to help with a programming crisis grew into a major commitment. That's a story for Book Five.

Then a series of hospital bills pushed me to the edge. Kevin came. My appendix got riled up. Elsie's chronic gall bladder problem demanded attention. Salary growth was minimal during the building program. When I learned of a school looking for a bus driver, I applied.

I fit morning and afternoon bus runs into my church work load and saw light at the end of the financial tunnel. All was well until one morning after my bus run, the principal summoned me. An unexpected influx of students had created a problem. Would I cover a seventh grade class between bus runs for a few days while he looked for a teacher? Days became weeks, the principal pulled me off the bus, and I became a substitute teacher.

Then there was Center Lake Camp. About the time we arrived, the Lower Michigan Conference began considering building a camp. The search for a site led to property a few miles south of Cadillac. I was on hand when the first tree fell. Wayside people joined work weekends, and when the camp became operational, numbers of our people attended adult retreats and we sent many campers to the summer program.

I volunteered one or more weeks each summer. During one of those weeks, the speaker was Lawrence Swanson, the pastor I had met at Camp Bird while serving the Iron River church. Since then, Lawrence had been called to lead the Baptist General Conference Bible School/Youth Board in Chicago. I admired Lawrence's spirit and skills with kids. The following year, I filled a one-year vacancy on his board. There will be occasion to look back on these encounters in the next chapters.

Our family enjoyed Muskegon and Wayside.

Elsie and the kids found good friends in the neighborhood, and the schools were excellent. The congregation continued to grow modestly, but in our fifth year progress slowed. I sensed some of the people were restless about my extra-curricular activity.

The Michigan district gathering was scheduled to meet in Algoma in May with Bill Turnwall as speaker. He was the BGC Home Missions Secretary and de facto bishop; the man restless pastors cozied up to at Bethel Founders Week.

Bill possessed a knack for making the smallest fish in the pond feel like a muskie. As I drove toward Algoma, I thought I might find opportunity for a discreet talk with him. At the first coffee break, I was pleased when Bill eased down beside me. But before I could speak I heard him say, "I just learned that Carl Lindman has resigned from Bethany in Anchorage. Would you consider going to Alaska?"

Eleven

ANCHORAGE
1958-1962

When Bill Turnwall asked if I would consider going to Alaska, I would like to report that I furrowed my brow and promised to give the matter much prayer. Truth is, I said yes almost before he was through speaking. I phoned Elsie and she graciously concurred.

Living in Alaska was a long-held dream. As long as I can remember, I had favored things north. I devoured Tarzan books but felt no urge to visit Africa. Southern bayous never lured me. But I loved everything Alaskan.

Elsie, on the other hand, was a city girl. A ritual exchange between us found her saying, "I never want to live in Alaska," and I would reply, "I never want to live in Chicago." Curiously, back-to-back assignments took us to both places. I am smugly grateful that Alaska came first.

Candidating for Alaska churches in those days involved phone conversations, a resume, family photos, and a taped sermon. The call came, and since the Bethany parsonage was furnished, we shipped only personal effects. I sold our rusting 1950 Chevy to an unfortunate teacher friend for

$100 and bought a used nine-passenger Ford station wagon. In mid-August we headed north.

Being romantically inclined and financially short, I decided we would camp on the way. Pitching a tent each night, sometimes in rain, proved less than romantic, yet the trip became a memorable family adventure.

At Dawson Creek, we reached the fabled Alaska Highway, 1,100 incredibly dusty miles to the Alaska border with near-blind turns, narrow bridges, and long stretches between services. Alcan horror stories abounded, but except for the dust and a chipped windshield, we had no problems.

Daylight hours lengthened as we drove north, allowing us to camp whenever weariness dictated. We reached Anchorage on the eighth day of travel. As we entered the city, illusions of frontier living faded. Apart from a distinct ruggedness, the businesses and neighborhoods we saw would fit in most northern towns. However, the Chugach Mountains looming to the east told us we were in Alaska.

Though my work changed little, suddenly we were missionaries. Our pictures appeared in Home Missions literature and women's groups sent pot holders and goodies at Christmas. I hoped the senders were remembering their pastor-missionaries at home with equal fervor.

The proliferation of churches in Anchorage surprised me. Most denominations were represented, plus a generous sprinkling of ministries launched by earnest freelancers and Gospel cowboys. I counted 20 Baptist churches.

Anchorage had four Baptist General Conference churches: Mountain View, Lake Spenard, Bethany, and Sand Lake, a new congregation meeting in a

Quonset hut on the city's rural fringe. Virgil Hegle came to Sand Lake shortly after we came to Bethany.

The BGC churches worked well together. We formed an inter-church council and organized as the Alaska Baptist Conference. Working with Home Missions, we helped establish a chapel and clinic at Sand Point, an island village off the Alaska Peninsula. Our churches touched a lot of people, but the regular rotation of military and business personnel dampened net growth. During our time at Bethany, we welcomed 54 new members and farewelled 56.

Bethany was a close-knit congregation. We held spontaneous picnics (when you get a pretty day, go for it). We visited Lazy Mountain Children's Home in Palmer. We took in a man and his son who had escaped from an Iron Curtain country. Several families headed to Bristol Bay each summer for commercial fishing. Book Two will tell many Alaska stories, including Elsie's longest walk.

My propensity for getting too involved continued unabated. I became publicity chair for the Anchorage annual evangelistic campaign. I edited a newsletter for the Alaska Baptist Conference. Victory Bible Camp at Glennallen and Solid Rock Bible Camp on the Kenai Peninsula caught my attention. The Alaska byline nudged editors to buy my stories and articles. To keep up with the mounting cost of living, I returned to substitute teaching. But the most demanding extra-curricular task was Anchorage Christian Youth (ACY), a Book Two story.

OUR ANCHORAGE STAY lasted only three years and four months, but Alaska captured our hearts.

When we moved to Chicago, Sally stayed behind to complete her senior year in high school. She lived with her friend, Mary Heynen, in the Christian Reformed parsonage.

While attending Bethel College later, Sally spent two summers working for the Alaska Department of Fish and Game. From 1968 to 1974 she and her husband, Dale, lived in Anchorage and Eagle River while Dale taught music in area schools. Their daughter, Gwen, was born during those years.

Joel attended the University of Alaska, Anchorage, and spent his entire teaching career at Lathrop High School in Fairbanks. During those years he had the good fortune to marry Sue, a Fairbanks newspaper woman.

For several years Joel's "Songs and Legends of Alaska" entertained tourists at Fairbanks' Polaris Hotel. He created a study skills workshop that served many kids in city and village schools.

Alaska lured me back often, usually to serve in camps. Those trips planted the seeds for our Wordshed Mission, a story for Chapter 15 and Book Five. I served Sand Lake Church as interim pastor for most of a year and spent the summer of 1998 in Egegik on Bristol Bay.

LOOKING BACK ON our years of ministry, I find the transitions of compelling interest. They hint of the web of providence. How was it that I drew the assignment to meet Lawrence Swanson's plane that rainy September afternoon in 1961? Usually, meeting planes was a festive, group affair. We had invited Lawrence to conduct leader training workshops for our BGC churches, and as Elsie and I drove him to his host's home, he confessed he did not feel well. He also confessed that a deadline distressed him. That deadline became the catalyst in the mix of providence that brought us to Chicago. Book Two will tell the story.

In October Lawrence called from Chicago to offer me a job as his assistant. I would direct boys work and camping and help him in other areas, particularly writing. The call jolted me: I did not know the job was open, and had I known, I would never have imagined myself as a candidate.

The offer was too challenging to resist, and Elsie and I agreed we should move. By mid-January I was sitting behind a desk in Conference headquarters staring at a folder labeled *Camping Guideposts.*

Twelve

Baptist General Conference
1962-1972

When Lawrence phoned about the headquarters job, he stressed the urgency of his need but did not explain. Though winter travel in Alaska can be precarious, I agreed to come in January.

Sixty below in Interior Alaska greeted the New Year, delaying our departure a few days, but when the weather moderated we loaded our Chevy wagon and pointed it toward Chicago.

Driving the snow-packed roads proved relatively comfortable. Traffic was light. In the Yukon Territory we rumbled over frozen rabbit carcasses—rabbits everywhere! We saw two lynx. The short winter days kept us driving mostly in darkness. We slept in cozy motels and ate in folksy restaurants. We encountered no travel problems until we reached Chicago. A heavy, wet snowfall had tied up the town and we got stuck.

We found an attractive apartment in Skokie ten miles north of headquarters. Lawrence put out an appeal for furnishings and the churches responded. Keith, Joel, David, and Kevin enrolled in school. We missed Sally. I began the commute through Chicago traffic to the BGC office at 5750 North Ashland.

On my desk when I arrived on the job lay a folder marked *Camping Guideposts*. It contained a sketchy outline and first chapter of a camp counselor handbook, the cause for Lawrence's urgency. Advertising was out and orders were piling up. Lawrence wanted the book by May. That was a tall order, almost impossible, considering the unanticipated distractions that ensued.

The first distraction was a two-week workshop tour of Nebraska for the National Sunday School Association, brought on by a family tragedy that wiped out the keynote speaker. Lawrence asked if I would go, and Elsie got her first taste of things to come. I was away from home far too often in the decade that followed.

The second distraction began when Martin Erickson, long-time editor of the BGC magazine, the *Standard,* fell sick. The Publications Department borrowed me to help part-time while he recovered, but he died. For a year I shuttled between offices. I learned that there is no such thing as part-time at an editor's desk.

To complicate things, spring rains flooded the lower level of our apartment, leading us to search for a house. We found a place in Prospect Meadows, twenty miles from my office

Writing in snatches and leaning on Lee Kingsley, our BGC camping guru, for ideas, I finished *Camping Guideposts* close to the target date. Lois Johnson, Lawrence's super secretary, typeset the pages on her Selectric. Harvest print shop ran a thousand copies, which I collated in my office and hauled to a binder in downtown Chicago. The book sold out in weeks, generating a story for Book Five.

Esther Larson, Martin Erickson's gifted long-time assistant, carried much of the *Standard* load, but the workload for me grew intense. When flu hit, I lacked the sense to ease off. One morning, I felt too sick to drive. Elsie took one look and hauled me to Swedish Covenant Hospital. The doctor declared I had a serious case of nephritis and slapped me in bed, where I stayed for two weeks.

Elsie visited each day. Colleagues sent funny get-well cards. A visiting youth pastor left with these cheering words: "God bless you, brother. My dad died of that." I noticed my absence did not shut down the magazine. I returned to the office well but not wise. Five years later another work-induced malady would put me in the hospital.

Finally, Don Anderson was chosen as editor. He spent the rest of his career at that post, raising the *Standard* to new levels of excellence.

Back full-time at my desk, Lawrence assigned me to work on a filmstrip. I wrote the script, recruited actors, hunted out filming locations, and worked with the production firm. I did almost everything except shoot the pictures and record the sound track.

I got to thinking about that. We had competent in-house photographers and I understood recording studio work. I proposed we make our own filmstrips and save substantial money, thus adding another layer of responsibility.

Christian Service Brigade units sprang up until BGC churches made up ten percent of the movement and I was invited to serve on the Brigade board of directors. Paul Nyberg, editor of Brigade's Venture for Boys, invited me to write a regular column, which I did for eight or nine years. Cap Matt became known to Brigade boys and leaders and invitations came to speak at Brigade functions across the land. I slept one night in Cap Matt's room at a lodge in northern Maine. Northwoods, Brigade's leadership camp in Michigan's Upper Peninsula, added me to its guest faculty list.

I sat with other camping executives on the National Sunday School Association Camping Commission. At one meeting, Graham Tinning, director of the Western Camp and Conference Association of California, shared his vision for a national camp leaders' organization. I found myself meeting at Wheaton College with key camping people, to lay the groundwork for Christian Camping International.

Camping Guideposts was the first Christian camping book distributed nationally. Moody Press picked it up after the first office edition sold out, opening the door for other camping books with several publishers.

I got involved with regional and national CCI conventions. The Canadian Sunday School Mission plugged me into its widespread camping outreach. In 1996 Elsie and I received the Kingsley Living Tribute Award for outstanding contribution to Christian camping. I count it a high privilege to have been part of the beginning of a significant movement that spread around the world.

IN 1965 I shifted gears. The BGC Men's Board set out to hire its first executive and someone tossed my name in the ring. I became the first (and last) Secretary of the Board of Men's Work. Following the structure of the Women's Board, I took boys work with me.

But I was ahead of the times. My philosophy of men's work closely paralleled the principles Promise Keepers would make famous years later, but hardly anyone noticed. They did notice our events for men at BGC annual conferences. A thousand men turned out for a wild game dinner in Duluth, the most memorable men's gathering the BGC would ever experience. Book Two will tell about that.

My Wilderness Trails program drew attention, too, not all of it positive. I set out to put a challenging wilderness experience within reach of every Conference man and boy. Some did not see canoe or backpack trips as "Christian" camping since there was no chapel.

Working with district camps, we helped put together trips in Maine, Washington, Oregon, Wyoming, and Minnesota. Book Three will tell about some of them.

But again the work load got out of hand. I developed a persistent cough that made speaking difficult. Rather than backing off, I set out on a series of BGC town meetings that wound up at Emmanuel Baptist in Duluth. My parents came to the meeting, and alarmed by my cough, they hauled me to a doctor. He peered down my throat and sent me home: paralyzed vocal cord.

Our Chicago doctor referred me to a specialist in Evanston. He put me in the hospital and ran every test known to mankind, including a bronchoscopy. He dug out a chunk for a biopsy. Finding nothing to cause my problem, he sent me to Rochester. A phalanx of white coats probed and pinched, gave my ailment a name and sent me home to live with it.

Not a happy prospect. I could speak softly but could not project my voice or sing. I checked in with our family doctor, who yanked on my tongue. Say aaaah. "I don't want to get your hopes up," he said, "but I think I detect movement. Let's turn it over to the Great Physician." The Great Physician smiled; my voice returned. I determined never again to be a hero.

In 1969 my job description changed again. The Men's, Women's, and Bible School/Youth Boards merged to form a Board of Christian Education and I was named Director of Adult Ministries, sort of a utility outfielder.

I sensed more change in the wind and restlessness crept over me. In the fall of 1971 I sent my resignation effective the end of December, rounding out ten good years at headquarters.

I am indebted to faithful office secretaries who made my work possible. So many colleagues blessed my days. A few still live as friends. How can I express my gratitude for Elsie and our kids, who lived without Dad far too many weeks?

I left Conference work with no sure destination, leading some friends to wonder if I was following God's will. I wondered too. Then my thoughts went back to the parable of Twisp Pass that gave my memoir its title: The trail is best discerned from the summit, looking back. Just head out and keep walking.

I wrote about that in my farewell piece in the *Standard*. Now, 38 years later, I have nary a doubt about my decision to resign.

Thirteen

THE BETWEEN YEARS
1972-1977

My resignation from Conference Headquarters in 1972 brought us midway through our 60 years of ministry. We began working together at the Union Gospel Mission during school years followed by pastorates in Wisconsin, Michigan, and Alaska. Next came ten years at Conference Headquarters.

When I left headquarters in 1972, I had a few free-lance assignments but no regular paycheck. Muttering the Lord will provide brings scant comfort to the lady who pays the bills, but the Lord did provide. Four short-term involvements in five years led ultimately to Duluth and North Shore Baptist, our final pastorate.

During those five years I worked briefly with Duane and Elsie Arvola, canoe outfitter friends from Babbitt, Minnesota. We explored the possibility of serving more churches and camps, which I saw as an extension of the wilderness emphasis I had pursued during Conference years. The idea didn't fly, but it led to a year with Soudan Baptist, a small church in an old mining community.

The church could not handle a full salary, and

I agreed to serve half time for a year while preparing to build at Whiteface Woods near Cotton on land my parents had given me.

Elsie remained in Illinois most of the summer of 1972 to provide a base for Kevin, who had just finished high school, and to sell our Prospect Meadows house. The sale gave us substantial funds for the first time in our marriage, making our home at Whiteface Woods possible.

In early 1974 we visited Dale and Sally in Alaska and made our first trips to Port Alsworth and Egegik, where we met Danny O'Hara and Paul and Nattie Boskoffsky, key figures in the Alaska Wordshed Mission books.

Two Finnish carpenters roughed in our Capp home in ten days and Elsie and I took on the finishing work, a marriage-straining chore. Lots of stories! I continued writing and travelling to supplement income from leader training programs we ran out of Whiteface Woods.

In 1974 Dale and Sally left Alaska and bought the Cotton Country Store. They moved into an apartment above the store and built up the business. They blessed the Cotton area in many ways.

In 1975 an invitation came from Camp Cedine, Spring City, Tennessee, to share in summer staff training and put together a promotional filmstrip. Dave was home from Indiana University and I took him along for company and to help with photography.

One Cedine trainee was Lila Sizemore from Columbus, Georgia. She and Dave found a lot to talk about. They kept in touch. By and by they invited me to marry them. The wedding would take place in Columbus on October 30, 1976.

It soon became apparent that our work at

Whiteface Woods would not sustain us. Weary of travel that would often leave Elsie home, I began to ponder options. When word came that Henry Harms, a friend from BGC days, had resigned as Christian education and camp director for the Iowa Baptist Conference, I contacted the district executive, also a BGC friend.

We met with district leadership in Davenport in early December. Elsie never forgot that trip—she slipped on a towel in our motel and broke her arm. The interview went favorably and in March 1976 we rented Whiteface Woods and moved to Eldora, Iowa, expecting to live there many years.

We found the house on camp property comfortable. We enjoyed social times with the executive minister and his wife. I helped build a small office building near our house to serve as a district and camp office. But as I visited among the churches, I found simmering tensions that had led my predecessor to resign after only two years. And as summer got under way, another disturbing factor arose.

On hot, still days, a nauseating stench drifted over the camp. I traced it to a tank in a ravine designed to hold overflow from the septic system during high-volume periods. But the tank also overflowed and each heavy rain carried our sewage into Pine Lake. Then I found that our kitchen greywater ran from the grease trap directly into the lake. We were a prime polluter! An inspector coming at the wrong time would shut us down in a heartbeat.

I was appalled to learn that the condition had been ignored for years because of the high cost for a remedy. The camp had other safety problems, but the pollution issue held priority. Continuing to ignore the problem was not an option for me, but when I pressed the matter with the executive, our relationship cooled.

I should have handled the issue with greater patience and diplomacy, but in my mind we were violating about everything Christian camping stood for. It became apparent that my boss and I were not on the same page when I heard him say to the board, "Lloyd and I have been discussing concerns we must address in two or three years."

Hope stirred briefly when a district fund drive was announced, but I was not granted input, and when fund goals were handed to our camp committee I hit the fan. The dollars allotted to the camp would not begin to address the sewer problem. I chewed on that for a while, and though I had been on the job only six months, I resigned.

My resignation included an offer to stay another six months to manage fall and winter retreats and lay groundwork for the next summer and to prioritize camp needs as I saw them. I was sure a documented, long-range plan would provide leverage for my successor, and that proved to be the case. My proposal was not helpful to the executive, but the district's political climate gave him little choice. And I needed time to explore our future.

While all this was unfolding, the date for Dave and Lila's wedding in Georgia drew near. I had saved vacation time and Elsie and I looked forward to the trip. But we could not have imagined what the next weeks would bring, or of the test of faith we would soon encounter. "The Tainted Fleece" in Book Two tells about that.

Fourteen

NORTH SHORE CHURCH
1977-1986

In March 1977 we moved from Iowa to the North Shore Church parsonage in Duluth. "The Tainted Fleece" in Book Two traces the unlikely path that led us there.

I felt a special kinship with the congregation, some of whom I had known from my youth. I thought often about my first visit on a snowy December Sunday in 1946. We rode in Dad's 1928 Chevrolet to a small, tarpaper-covered house on Brighton Street. He shuffled through loose snow to clear a path for Mother and me. He carried his Bible in one hand and a bucket of coal in the other. While he fired up the stove, Mother swept away snow that had filtered in around the windows. Soon kids and a few adults circled the stove and Sunday school began.

From that humble beginning, North Shore Church evolved. More of the story in Book Two.

The fellowship prospered in the chapel house and built an attractive new church on Lakewood Road near the lake. Pastor John Olson's ten-year ministry strengthened the congregation but in the mid-'70s it entered a period of decline. When two neighboring churches got to squabbling, several families migrated to North Shore, and we found a gregarious mix of young and old who were open to leadership.

Elsie and I felt comfortable among the people and I practiced the cardinal rules for pastoring: love the people, preach the Word, and pay attention to kids. North Shore people were easy to love.

After about a year, thinking the congregation might tolerate me until retirement, I sought permission to buy a house. We began the search in mid-summer, but finding a home in our price range and community of choice proved frustrating. Fall turned to winter, and we agreed to postpone the house search until spring.

On a Thursday in early March I settled at my desk for a rare, quiet evening of reading. Elsie was on a night shift assignment from the nursing bureau she worked with. The phone rang. I was mildly annoyed to hear Elsie ask if I would look at one more house.

Out of habit, she had scanned the want ads. She spotted a home for sale by owner in Lester Park, our area of choice. She called the number in the ad. The owner said he was showing the house that evening and would welcome another prospect. The address was 5118 Glendale Street, about six blocks from my ancestral Oneida Street home.

Slipping into my jacket to face a sloppy evening, I was certain I would not like the house. The phone rang again. A gravelly voice said, "Just wanted to be sure you were coming." Pushy, I thought.

I drove the familiar neighborhood to a blue, hip-roofed house with a beamed living room and south-facing picture window. A blue flood lit a circle of young spruce in the back yard. I liked the house immediately. The price was right. I asked the owner when I could bring my wife by and he suggested noon the next day.

I had spotted a phone on the kitchen wall and picked it up to confer with Elsie. The phone was dead. Puzzled, I asked the owner if he had called me. No, a lady had reached him at his new home, but she gave no name or number.

Dread crept slowly over me. Thursday! I had completely forgotten an appointment with the Sunday school staff at Bethany Baptist, 10 miles away. I told the owner to look for us at noon the next day and sped off.

That was just the beginning of remarkable events surrounding the house we have lived in for 30 years. "This Old House" in Book Two tells the story.

WE VACATED THE parsonage just in time to stave off mutiny in the church. The building provided only two, single-occupancy washrooms, and each Sunday morning an impatient line formed outside the women's washroom. There seemed no solution short of building additional space, and the congregation was leery of debt. Then the parsonage sale provided considerable equity.

We engaged an architect and hired Odin Alreck to rough in the building. Odin was a rough-hewn, skilled contractor. He and his wife, Joan, attended North Shore, but Odin vowed he would never join a church—he had seen too much.

Oden improved on the architect's plan and brought the building to the finishing state. Then he ramrodded volunteers to complete it. Eighteen months after groundbreaking, we had a handsome 3,000-square foot, two-story addition with a nursery, library, classrooms, fireside room overlooking Lake Superior, and two spacious, bright washrooms. The building was paid for, and Oden was the first person to be baptized in the newly appointed baptistery.

Dedication Sunday gave me one of the most moving encounters of my life, a hug from Sister Noami, a Benedictine nun. Another story for Book Two.

NORTH SHORE SPONSORED teen canoe trips and kids camps at nearby Camp Green Hill. We enjoyed RV caravans and winter weekends at primitive Mink Lake Camp. We got involved in Indian ministry.

We reached out to the community. Long-time friend Stanley Lindholm and I led Wednesday morning chapels at Park Point Manor for seven years. We took part in St. Luke's on-call chaplain program. I produced about 2,000 five-minute North Country Notebook broadcasts on WWJC Radio. We soon tripled our missions budget and we helped Lorraine Green, North Shore's first missionary, on her way to Chad.

A warm memory carries me back to the Duluth airport as Lorraine came home for her first furlough. Kids and adults clustered around their missionary with balloons, flowers, laughter and hugs, true church filled with joy and love, and I was privileged to be its pastor. I cried.

We held no evangelistic campaigns and organized no visitation programs, yet we grew. A young man confessed faith in Christ during marriage counseling. I sat with an older friend close to a barrel stove on a cold January day at Camp Green Hill and heard him ask, "Pastor, what does it mean to be a Christian?"

Josh and the turtle. Gene and the Green Hill fish fry. Charlie's lost choppers. Tim, the midnight bugler. See Book Two.

Elsie and I grew closer. For too many years my travels had separated us. Now we traveled together. We bought a pop-up travel trailer, then a Scamp camper. One vacation trip to Texas and the East Coast led us into a publishing venture we had never imagined. An unplanned, extended stay in Alaska gave rise to our Wordshed Mission that thus far has sent out 26,000 books.

After nine good years with people we loved, we took early retirement, leaving behind a healthy congregation with money in the bank. Over the next years we were saddened to watch the fellowship fade and finally die. But one North Shore chapter was yet to be written, a story for the final chapter.

Fifteen

THE CLOSING YEARS
1986-2002

My primary reason for early retirement was to get at stories that had churned in my belly ever since the summer of 1979 when Danny O'Hara told his life story at North Shore Church. I knew someday I had to write his story.

I knew how to write stories and how publish books, but I did not know where the money would come from. Leaving funding with the Lord, we set up the Wordshed Mission. Our start-up goal was two Alaska titles.

Ratcheting up research, I began to work on my subjects to let me tell their stories, not a simple task. I had been collecting Alaska material for years, good stuff, but I needed to get the particulars. The first book would record the story of Don and Lorene Stump.

The distribution plan was simple: I would give half the press run to the subjects to use as they wished and spread the rest around as a witness to God's grace. The proceeds of any books sold would go back into the Mission fund. I knew that would make for slow going, but then I stumbled on a stash of free money.

WITH MY MIND on publishing, I had not given much thought to interim pastorates, a common occupation for geezer preachers, though I did Sunday preaching now and then.

Circumstances had taken us back to Whiteface Woods, and Emmanuel Baptist of Virginia, just up the road, invited me to come for a Sunday. Their pastor had just left. We had a good time and the church asked if I would consider serving as interim pastor. They wanted Sunday through Wednesday and I could commute from home. I accepted the invitation.

I would spend 16 rewarding months with Emmanuel, my longest interim. During that period, we moved back to our home on Glendale Street. Almost immediately, a call came from the BGC church in Ironwood. Over the next 16 years, I would serve interim situations in four states. I served 11 churches (some twice), one camp, and a fishing village on Bristol Bay in Alaska. Tenures averaged about eight months.

Work continued on Wordshed Mission goals, and now I had funding. Since my minister's pension and Social Security met household needs, I could invest interim stipends in the books.

Book Five will tell the Wordshed Mission story. Quite a ride! Generous gifts from friends and relatives along with interim stipends allowed us to print 26,500 copies of four Wordshed titles and turn two titles into audio books.

This memoir series will probably be Wordshed's last gasp, adding six titles and 6,000 books. On the drawing board, a multi-copy, digital story supplement and DVD photo album.

Recalling the interim years brings mixed feelings. Joy for many blessings, but sadness at the pain I witnessed. Most churches I served had been wounded, some badly, by leadership bent on new ways of doing church. Pastors, mostly young men, sacrificed people who had poured their lives into their church. You can't plant California seeds in northern hinterlands. I don't know of one instance where this succeeded, and rarely does a church regain the level from which it fell. Pastors move on while leaving bitterness in the people's hearts and wreckage in their wake.

But interims brought much joy. I loved the people, preached the Word, and had fun with the kids. That is the only way to build a church. I came with no agenda but to prepare the congregation for a new pastor. I spent my time calming troubled waters, rounding up stray sheep, and thinking up ways to have Sunday fun with kids. Book Two will tell kid's time stories.

Interims brought conversions, baptisms, child dedications, weddings, and funerals. We burned two mortgages, tackled neglected building repairs, and revived a moribund building program. Once I jury-rigged a recording studio in the parsonage kitchen to fix an incredibly bad Sunday morning broadcast.

It was a privilege to be interim director for Lake Ellen Camp in Michigan's Upper Peninsula. I had helped put together the first camp week, 40 Brigade boys and men in Army surplus tents. Some of the men were still around. You will meet one in Book Four, "The Society."

Almost every interim brought situations or

people that my life experiences had equipped me to serve. I gained enduring friendships and blessed memories.

Then, poignantly, our interim years ended where they had begun.

Sixteen

SUNSET AND EVENING STAR
2002-

In 2002 I eased back on interims. I gave more time to writing and Elsie made her way to the golf course, but less and less often. Arthritis was taking a toll on her back and hands. On the last Sunday of 2002 we drove to Emmanuel Baptist of Virginia to preach at Sunday morning worship. We met old friends and reminisced about my first interim 16 years earlier.

Four of those friends, Bob and Sharon Anderson and Dale and Janet Skinner, invited Elsie and me to the Lord Stanley Restaurant in Eveleth. They went ahead to find a table.

It was a sloppy day and I dropped Elsie off at the restaurant door while I parked. I paused in the restroom, talked for several minutes with a tourist and then gave my attention to the buffet. My friends and Elsie already had their food.

When I joined them, I noticed that Elsie looked flustered. I learned she had fallen. As she returned from the buffet with her tray, her chair, on casters, flew out behind her and she landed hard, bumping her head on the chair, which had wedged against the wall.

The men leaped to assist her, and Elsie felt mostly embarrassed. Her head hurt some, but nothing else, she said. The waitress witnessed the fall and offered assistance, but Elsie reported no serious discomfort. I carelessly failed to report the accident to the restaurant manager.

As we drove home, I quizzed Elsie about pain. She attributed some soreness to encroaching spinal arthritis earlier X rays had revealed. But back discomfort and pain in her right leg intensified. One morning, as Elsie chopped vegetables at the kitchen counter, crippling pain shot through her right leg. X rays and a CT scan revealed a damaged spinal disk. Weeks of treatment followed, but spinal injections and physical therapy brought no relief. Severe arthritis made surgery too risky, and treatment focused on pain management.

Careful positioning in the bed brought temporary relief, and I became a full-time caregiver. Recognizing that Elsie's injury was permanent, I took a reverse mortgage to finance remodeling to meet her needs. The family provided personal and financial support. Medicare and Blue Cross picked up doctor and hospital costs but not the costly medications.

I sought compensation for remodeling expenses, but the insurer denied liability. The attorney wheedled $5,000 for a disclaimer of future claims. Remodeling costs reached $15,000 and climbing.

We gratefully accepted the offer of Kevin and his wife, Tena, to leave their careers to live with us and share in Elsie's care. Dave and Lila came to guide remodeling. Keith recruited a carpenter and electrician from his contacts in Chisholm. Sally and Dale, who had moved to Duluth some time before, lent faithful support. Joel and Sue contributed a TV for our room and a quality adjustable bed to replace the miserable hospital bed Medicare provided. Our kids, grandkids, and others sent generous contributions.

Shortly after we bought the house, I converted the attached garage into a family room. We turned that into our quarters. Dave raised the floor six inches and installed bi-fold doors into the living room. Two wardrobes set off a six-by-12-foot space for my work space.

Dave relocated the front door and worked the former hall and powder room into a full bath with space for a handicap-access four-foot shower. Keith's volunteers did the carpentry and wiring. Keith's daughter Amy and her husband, George, came from Elyria, Ohio, to install the shower.

I watched Elsie regress from cane to walker to wheelchair; from bathroom to commode. Reaction to medications sent us repeatedly to ER and the hospital to adjust her blood chemistry. Once I had to ambulance her to St. Mary's.

Five hospital stays and two extended periods in residential therapy treatments brought no relief. Then, signs of dementia began to appear. A fall and slight stroke ended the second residential therapy.

Our St. Mary's social worker helped secure home care, but Elsie continued to fade. Her misery exacerbated the dementia and our good doctor Nisswandt enrolled Elsie in hospice for pain control.

Soon it became apparent that we could no longer safely care for her at home, and on October 31, 2007, we entered Chris Jensen Health Care

Center. In spite of her weakness and confusion, Elsie was aware of the transition. When the hard time came to tell her that Chris Jensen would be our new home, she added, clearly and simply, "and our new ministry." Those were prophetic words.

AS A PASTOR I have stood by many spouses separated by age or illness to bring what comfort I could. Now I was on the receiving end. Elsie's misery had forced us to give up church attendance, and I would not think of attending without her, yet one hungers for a caring fellowship. The Lord met that need in a remarkable way.

I had watched my beloved congregation shrink as pastor-people relationships grew increasingly brittle. One Sunday, 60 years after North Shore began as a Sunday school mission in a tarpaper-covered house on Brighton Street, a failed pastor, instead of resigning, gathered 16 remaining members and dissolved the church. The Minnesota Baptist Conference took ownership and began negotiations to sell the property.

Following the dissolution, a small group clustered around a young mother who was working through cancer treatment. They gained permission to meet in the Fireside Room Sunday mornings while the sale was being negotiated. Oden Alreck phoned and asked if I could help.

The love shown by old and new friends and the informal setting in a room I had helped build overlooking the lake wonderfully met our needs. With help, Elsie could still climb stairs. We called ourselves North Shore Chapel and based our fellowship on the first church: "They devoted themselves to the apostles teaching and to the fellowship, to the breaking of bread and to prayer." (Acts 2:42).

When Hermantown Community Church bought the building, our chapel group met for a few weeks in a restaurant, but the space was cold and uninviting, and Bob and Carol Bacon invited us to meet in their home on Brighton Street, not far from a trim building that 60 years before was an empty, tarpaper-covered house.

Epilogue

Well, that's all the years of my life, but the good stuff is yet to come. Lord willing, I'll put together four storybooks covering all the years, plus an old man's rambling confession of faith.

At this writing, Elsie still lingers, a mite of 75 pounds. She still knows us and responds with an occasional sentence. She lives in the twilight of powerful pain meds. We walk the halls during her few waking hours, touching lives as we walk.

I am awed and humbled by the fulfillment of Elsie's prophetic words as we entered the nursing home 14 months ago. When I told her this would be our new home, she replied, "and our new ministry." Book Two will tell the story.

When I look at the list of stories this book promised and stories set aside for Books Three and Four, it is evident the books will not hold them and stay within 96 pages. Therefore, relying on digital marvels I do not understand, I will record *The Oracles of Great-Grandpa Lloyd.*

This is a noble pursuit, for until Guttenberg invented the printing press, mankind's (and God's) only means for preserving and sharing information was the storyteller, the oracle.

All the Days of My Life has been a family enterprise. Keith, Sr. shot the photos and designed the covers. Joel's wife, Sue, edited the manuscript and designed and typeset the pages. Joel repaired old Dad's memory and Sally and Dale did final proofing and made helpful suggestions. Dave and Kevin lent recollections, encouragement, and technical skills.

North Shore Chapel, the church at Bob and Carol's house, adopted the project and lent financial help. Scores of friends sent gifts. Steve Krueger and his crew at Arrow Printing in Bemidji did their usual outstanding work.

All the Days of My Life has been soul therapy through the days and long nights of Elsie's slow decline. How can I thank family and friends for their kindness and prayers? And hospice and Chris Jensen professionals for gentle care for Elsie and me. They knew when I needed a hug.

Warning: Book Six will dismay some readers. I make no apology for offending tradition. We serve the God of all grace, whose Person, mercy, and works transcend the farthest reach of human imagination.